TIMOTHY

PRIORITES OF PASTORAL LEADERSHIP

Study by Lance Wallace
Commentary by Guy Sayles

Free downloadable Teaching Guide for this study available at
NextSunday.com/teachingguides

NextSunday Resources
6316 Peake Road
Macon, Georgia 31210-3960
1-800-747-3016
©2021 by NextSunday Resources
All rights reserved.

TABLE OF CONTENTS

Timothy: Priorities of Pastoral Leadership

HOW TO USE THIS STUDY

NextSunday Resources Adult Bible Studies are designed to help adults study Scripture seriously within the context of the larger Christian tradition and, through that process, find their faith renewed, challenged, and strengthened. We study the Scriptures because we believe they affect our current lives in important ways. Each study contains the following three components:

Study Guide

Each study guide lesson is arranged in four movements:

Reflecting recalls a contemporary story, anecdote, example, or illustration to help us anticipate the session's relevance in our lives.

Studying is centered on giving the biblical material in-depth attention while often surrounding it with helpful insights from theology, ethics, church history, and other areas.

Understanding helps us find relevant connections between our lives and the biblical message.

What About Me? provides brief statements that help unite life issues with the meaning of the biblical text.

Commentary

Each study guide lesson is accompanied by an additional, in-depth commentary on the biblical material. Written by a different author than the study guide, each commentary gives the opportunity for learners to approach the Scripture text from a separate but complementary viewpoint.

Teaching Guide

In addition to the provided study guide and commentary, *NextSunday Resources* also provides a *free* downloadable teaching guide, available at NextSunday.com. Each teaching guide gives the teacher tools for focusing on the content of each study guide lesson through additional commentary and Bible background information. Through teacher helps and teaching options, each teaching guide also provides substance for variety and choice in the preparation of each lesson.

NextSunday
Resources

STUDY INTRODUCTION

First Timothy is the first of three so-called "Pastoral Epistles" attributed to the Apostle Paul. The letter is called "pastoral" because the author offers guidance to Timothy, a young minister facing daunting pastoral challenges in his church. It provides a strikingly relevant look into building up believers and growing a church today. As we study 1 Timothy, we will address teaching and understanding the Bible, the character expected of a leader, training to be an example to others, and building relationships based on mutual respect.

It's important to understand, however, that this letter isn't only for pastors. All who participate in the life of the church need to become better students of the Bible, members of a local congregation, and followers of Christ. Be open to how these texts speak to you. As you grapple with them, let your own personal journey be informed.

This unit is also a good opportunity to give laypeople the chance to "peek behind the curtain" and see what church leadership really looks like. The more open we are to the text, the guidance of the Holy Spirit, and the insights of our fellow group members, the more likely that this will be a transformative experience for us all.

1

SOUND
FAITH

1 Timothy 1: 1-9b

Central Question

What does sound faith look like?

Scripture

1 Timothy 1:1-9b

1 From Paul, who is an apostle of Jesus Christ by the command of God our savior and of Christ Jesus our hope. 2 To Timothy, my true child in the faith. Grace, mercy, and peace from God the Father and from Christ Jesus our Lord. 3 When I left for Macedonia, I asked you to stay behind in Ephesus so that you could instruct certain individuals not to spread wrong teaching. 4 They shouldn't pay attention to myths and endless genealogies. Their teaching only causes useless guessing games instead of faithfulness to God's way of doing things. 5 The goal of instruction is love from a pure heart, a good conscience, and a sincere faith. 6 Because they missed this goal, some people have been distracted by talk that doesn't mean anything. 7 They want to be teachers of Law without understanding either what they are saying or what they are talking about with such confidence. 8 Now we know that the Law is good if used appropriately. 9 We understand this: the Law isn't established for a righteous person but for people who live without laws and without obeying any authority. They are the ungodly and the sinners.

Reflecting

Jaime Escalante became a household name in the late 1980s after the release of the film *Stand and Deliver* (Warner Brothers, 1988), in which actor Edward James Olmos portrayed Escalante's success teaching mathematics at Garfield High School in East Los Angeles. In the film and in other works depicting his methods, Escalante made it clear that teaching math and helping students to pass the Advanced Placement exam in calculus was not his main instructional objective. His true goal was to give poor and underestimated Latino students hope for themselves and faith in their abilities. He famously focused his curriculum around the concept of unlocking the students' desire to learn. His one criticism of the film was that it did not accurately depict how hard the students had to work.

Escalante was so successful that in 1982, all eighteen of his students passed the Advanced Placement exam, causing testing officials to suspect them of cheating (Sanchez, NPR). They retook the exam, passed again, and proved the accusations—which were based on nothing more than racism and suspicion—to be false.

In this letter to his protégé, Timothy, Paul dispenses advice on teaching and leading. In this opening section, he reveals his true instructional objective: "The goal of instruction is love from a pure heart, a good conscience, and a sincere faith" (1 Tim 1:5). For the church at Ephesus, the stakes were much higher than passing an exam. Their discipleship depended on sound teaching from an authentic and pure source. Sound faith comes from sound teaching, and both can be hard to find.

Studying

Much debate and scholarship has gone into establishing the authorship of the pastoral letters (1–2 Timothy and Titus). Traditionally, they are attributed to the Apostle Paul and said to have been written some time after the events recorded in the book of Acts. Many scholars, however, point to discrepancies in Greek language and style, church structure, and theological themes between these letters and the undisputed letters of Paul such as Romans and Galatians. These scholars would say the pastoral letters were written after Paul's death by someone who hoped to express Paul's teaching to a later generation.

The term "pastoral epistles" is somewhat of a misnomer since Timothy was not the pastor of the church at Ephesus. He was acting in a pastoral role, however, and Paul was certainly being pastoral in his instructions to Timothy. Timothy's role in Ephesus was comparable to having a guest evangelist or missionary stay at your church for several months to preach, lead Bible studies, hold meetings with church leaders, and engage with those leaders in one-on-one conversations.

Timothy was a trusted co-laborer in Paul's missionary endeavors. He is frequently mentioned in Acts and in several of Paul's letters. In the first letter to the church at Thessalonica, Paul suggests that Timothy should be ranked among the apostles (Ciholas, 920).

Despite the frequent references to Timothy throughout the New Testament, not much is known about his background. We can glean from 2 Timothy that his family was ethnically mixed. His mother, Eunice, and grandmother, Lois, were Jewish believers and followers of Christ. The fact that they had Greek names indicates they participated in Greek culture to some degree, perhaps at the insistence of Timothy's father, who is unnamed in Scripture (Ciholas, 920). Timothy is first mentioned in Acts 16 in relation to a controversy around circumcision. He's forbidden from participating in Paul's missionary efforts because he was not circumcised. Timothy fulfilled this Jewish ritual, however, in order to become a Christian missionary, an irony that would make him intimately acquainted with harsh teachings that could divide churches.

As a participant in Paul's ministry, Timothy was often a messenger. In Acts, he might either precede or follow up on a visit from Paul to a local body of believers. Acts 17 tells how he remained behind in Beroea with Silas. Acts 19 mentions that he and Erastus went to Macedonia ahead of Paul's visit. First Thessalonians 3 refers to Timothy's presence with the church at Thessalonica, which was undergoing tremendous persecution. Timothy was also involved in trying to correct the problems experienced by the church at Corinth.

In a way, Timothy was the first traveling church consultant, assisting local churches as they dealt with issues that hindered their growth and God's mission. Although he is often referred to as a pastor, and much of the content of 1 Timothy deals with the qualifications for church leadership, his ministry as described in Scripture is more transient and temporary, visiting local congregations for a brief time before moving on.

Paul sent Timothy to Ephesus to address the problem of false teaching. The specific nature of this teaching is never stated, however—a fact that is both puzzling and helpful. On one hand, this lack of information is puzzling because our curiosity is sparked by phrases such as "myths and genealogies" (v. 4). It's natural to want to understand what Paul was talking about so we can apply the Bible's teaching accurately. It is likely that the false teaching was related to an interpretation of Jewish law (Polhill, 649), but it is only described in the text in such general terms as "ruined their faith" (1:19) and "consciences will be seared" (4:2). We also know from Paul's exhortation that this false teaching was causing divisions among believers.

At the same time, it can be helpful not to know too much about the false teachers. How so? For one thing, it makes us focus instead on the *effects* of the teaching and seek to avoid these effects in our leadership and teaching. Whatever it's specific content, we can be sure Paul would have churches set aside those disagreements to focus on the most central elements of the faith.

Second, it makes us focus instead on our *response* to this teaching. Timothy's role in Ephesus was to confront the false teaching and call attention to its devastating effects. Leadership has a responsibility to name the causes of dissension in order to address them.

Finally, the lack of detail forces us to focus instead on our *approach to Scripture*. There are ways of handling the Bible that Paul calls "useless" (v. 4). We sometimes fall into a trap of believing that any Bible study is helpful. Paul insists that without a pure motive for teaching and a proper understanding of the journey of faith, a misguided or misleading interpretation of Scripture will harm a congregation.

Paul also emphasizes that though the law may be at the root of the problem, the law itself is not harmful. He is walking a fine line to keep from alienating Jewish believers who perhaps would have been struggling to reconcile Jewish practices with Christian teaching. He states in verse 8 that the Law is good "if used appropriately." He doesn't want Timothy to tip the scales in the other direction in favor of the Greek or Gentile believers and thus send Jewish believers running for the exits. The situation in Ephesus required a delicate balance, not unlike many of the congregations with whom Paul worked and many troubled churches today.

Beneath the surface of this opening exhortation is a strong undercurrent of genuine love and concern. Paul wants the church at Ephesus to exhibit sound faith and not succumb to distracting arguments.

Understanding

Have you ever listened to a sermon or participated in a Bible study group during which a well-intentioned preacher or teacher said something that didn't sit well with you? We might chalk that up to "being under conviction" or "learning a new truth." In reality, it could have been the Holy Spirit offering a gentle warning.

Or suppose the roles were reversed. Maybe you were the one leading the Bible study or sharing your thoughts about some religious matter. Later, you came to see that what you had said came from a place of personal interpretation rather than careful reading led by the Holy Spirit. How did it make you feel to find you may have led others astray? Dishonest? Embarrassed? Did you question your motives?

Timothy was sent to help the church at Ephesus establish a foundation of sound faith. Paul's confrontation with the false teaching is aimed at getting those erring in their interpretation of Scripture and Christian practice to consider their motives. If they led out of love, they would receive Timothy's correction and forsake their divisive instruction. Love is the simple yet profound corrective to bad church leadership. The problem is that so often the teacher leading people into confusion and disharmony doesn't understand what he or she is doing, or why. Admittedly, confronting such teaching involves walking a difficult tightrope, but Paul's love for the believers in Ephesus drove him to urge Timothy to stand up to the problem teachers.

This type of confrontation is largely absent from churches today. Why is that? Maybe we aren't confident in our own grasp of Scripture. Maybe we are too tolerant of other interpretations, even when they cause harm. We have to focus on the results of the teaching, however. Spiritual discernment is not so difficult or mystical that we can't possibly know when the church is unhealthy. We simply have to see what is happening. Is the body of Christ being uplifted and brought together or is it being torn apart by trivial matters? And who gets to decide what is trivial? These questions are the real challenges of today's text.

What About Me?

• *Being a good learner.* Before Timothy could accomplish his mission, he had to learn from Paul's teaching and his example. As we think about our own ministry within the church, let us approach Scripture with humility and hunger for understanding. Let us pay attention to our own spiritual foundation before we attempt to teach others.

• *Being a good teacher.* Sound teaching comes from love, a pure conscience, and sincere faith. This is a powerful three-point checklist we can use to diagnose our own teaching and leadership. Are we teaching out of obligation? Do we need to hold power over others? Do we need to be in control? Are we susceptible to ego? Be self-aware. Ask yourself where your desire for leadership comes from and pray for the Holy Spirit's assistance to stay true to these three principles.

> When does a simple difference of opinion cross the line into "false doctrine"? How should Christians who are concerned about both love and truth respond when this happens?

• *Discerning good teaching from bad.* How can we tell good teaching from bad? By looking at the outcome. Does the teaching build up the church? Then it is coming from love, a pure conscience, and sincere faith. Does the teaching create confusion and division? Then it is not from God. Paul's words to Timothy clarify what could be a difficult problem to sort out. In this case, discernment is about applying simple but profound principles that are as true now as in Timothy's day.

• *Correcting bad teaching.* Timothy's mission was to root out unhealthy and unhelpful teaching, but it would be no easy feat for him to accomplish the task Paul had given him. Addressing unhealthy teaching is a necessary aspect of church leadership, even if it is sometimes stressful and unpleasant. In Galatians 6:1, Paul advised believers to restore the errant with "a spirit of gentleness." If we approach someone with questions rather than accusations, we have a better chance of helping that person recognize his or her errors.

Resources

James L. Blevins, "Ephesus," *Mercer Dictionary of the Bible*, ed. Watson E. Mills et al. (Macon GA: Mercer University Press, 1990).

Paul Ciholas, "Timothy," *Mercer Dictionary of the Bible*, ed. Watson E. Mills et al. (Macon GA: Mercer University Press, 1990).

John B. Polhill, "Pastoral Epistles," *Mercer Dictionary of the Bible*, ed. Watson E. Mills et al. (Macon GA: Mercer University Press, 1990).

Claudio Sanchez, "Jaime Escalante's Legacy: Teaching Hope," *National Public Radio*, 31 March 2010 <http://www.npr.org/templates/story/story.php?storyId=125398451>.

SOUND FAITH

1 Timothy 1:1-9b

Unhelpful Distinctions between "Clergy" and "Laity"

We begin today a four-lesson unit from 1 Timothy on the priorities of pastoral leadership. Most of the teachers of these lessons, like most of people who will gather to study them, are not pastors. For that reason, the relevance of these lessons may not be immediately clear. Why should "laypeople" study texts like these? There are many reasons.

In churches that affirm the priesthood of all believers, distinctions between laity and clergy aren't absolute. They may not even be helpful. The differences are more about roles and function than about status and responsibility. When I played high school football, I was an offensive tackle. Unlike my teammates who scored touchdowns, my name never appeared in any reports about our games. That didn't mean I was less important than the running backs and pass receivers, just less noticed— although the best quarterbacks and running backs knew how much they depended on linemen. Pastoral leaders do get recognized more often than those with different kinds of ministries, but that doesn't mean pastoral leaders are more important.

There aren't "first-class" and "second-class" Christians, a truth that applies not only to status in a church but also to responsibility. Though a church's designated pastors and ministers have a greater degree of *accountability* for areas of ministry, such as leading worship, nurturing faith through teaching, providing pastoral care, and exercising overall leadership, *responsibility* for the overall health and faithfulness of the church rests with all its members.

It's also true that laity have callings to ministries within and beyond the church. These ministries enhance the ability of the church to carry out its mission. Such ministries have significant pastoral dimensions that call for the people who perform them to have the same personal qualities we want our pastors to have. Especially when it comes to respectable character, heartfelt compassion, and genuine commitment to the common good, laypeople have hopes for themselves that aren't very different from their hopes for their pastors and ministers. Certainly the consequences of failing to meet such standards are higher for clergy, since their failures affect so many others, but the essence of those standards applies to all the "believer-priests" in a church.

Background of the Pastoral Epistles

Another reason these lessons on pastoral leadership are important for everyone is that all of us have pastors for whom we have expectations and upon whose guidance and care we depend. This unit of study gives us an opportunity to evaluate our expectations in light of what the early church thought were important traits and skills of pastors.

So, these lessons offer important insights for laity and clergy alike. First Timothy is one of the three "Pastoral Epistles" in the New Testament. Second Timothy and Titus are the others. We're not exactly sure about the chronological order in which they were written. They're arranged in our Bibles according to their length.

There are also some questions about who wrote these letters. Though the Apostle Paul is named as the author in all three, it wasn't uncommon in the first century for students of well-known teachers to write in their names. Since these letters describe developments of both theology and church structure that likely emerged after Paul died, many scholars think someone whom Paul influenced wrote them. Other commentators doubt that anyone other than Paul could have written them, since they contain very personal comments by Paul to Timothy (1 Tim 1:2; 4:14; 5:23; 2 Tim 4:6-21) and Titus (3:12-13). My view is that Paul wrote to (and possibly spoke with) Timothy and Titus about many of the concerns these letters address, and that his instructions were expanded and shaped into the final written form sometime late in the first or very early in the second century (see James D. G. Dunn, "First and Second Letters to Timothy," *The New Interpreter's Bible*, vol. 11 [Nashville TN: Abingdon, 2000] 780, n. 22). Whoever wrote them, and in whatever way, the early church received the guidance of the Pastoral Epistles as a gift from Paul.

These letters are addressed to individuals who offer pastoral leadership for the church: in Timothy's case, for the church (or community of churches) in Ephesus (1 Tim 1:3). As we'll see, Paul offered encouragement and instruction for faithful ministry that would result in "sound teaching" for the church (1:11) and "honor and glory" for God (1:17). Although Paul wrote these letters to Timothy and Titus, the ending of each letter indicates that they were read to the congregations because the "you" in these closing words is plural.

The Importance of "Fathers" and "Mothers" in Faith

Paul begins 1 Timothy's letter with an affirmation that he did the work of an apostle in obedience to "the command of God our savior and of Christ Jesus our hope" (1:1) and with an affectionate reference to Timothy as his "true child in the faith" (1:2).

Timothy, who was considerably younger than Paul, had labored side by side with Paul for many years (Acts 16:1-3; 1 Thess 3:2-6). Paul once commended him to the troubled church in Corinth, writing, "I've sent Timothy to you; he's my loved and trusted child in the Lord" (1 Cor 4:17; see also Phil 2:19-22). Paul had been instrumental in nurturing Timothy's faith and training him for ministry. Paul was a father figure and mentor to him.

In my work with seminary students, I've seen how important it is for them to have "fathers and mothers" in the faith, people who are invested in more than (not less than!) their academic achievement. They need and want people who take an interest in their practice of the faith, not simply their *understanding* of it. They need and want people who invest in their growth as followers of Jesus, not merely in their effectiveness as ministers who serve the church. In other words, they want what we all want: someone to love us enough to encourage us to deepen our love for Jesus.

God's Way of Doing Things

Timothy stayed behind in Ephesus when Paul left for Macedonia (1:3; see Acts 20:13-38). Paul's departure meant that primary leadership of the church became Timothy's responsibility.

One of his first tasks was to stop the spread of a particular form of "wrong teaching" (1:3) that was focused on "myths and endless genealogies" and led to "useless guessing games instead of faithfulness to God's way of doing things" (1:4). The "myths" were most likely the stories of the gods found in Greek and Roman mythologies. The "genealogies" were likely fanciful symbolic interpretations of the ancient family trees found in the book of Genesis.

The kind of teaching the church needed was about "faithfulness to God's way of doing things" (1:4). Understanding this phrase is important to our interpretation of 1 Timothy. "God's way of doing things" refers to how God puts things in order. In Ephesus, as in all the places where Roman and Greek ways of viewing reality had great influence, it was common to think of governance as overseeing and managing a "house."

The Greek word for house (or family) is *oikos*, from which get the words *ecology* and *economics*. In the Greco-Roman world, regional governments and even the empire as a whole were thought of as a kind of household. Such use of the word house survives today in terms such as "House of Representatives" and "courthouse." When I was a boy, some of the older folks called our sanctuary the "meeting house" or the "church-house." In this letter, Paul told Timothy that a qualification for pastoral leaders is their ability to "manage their...household[s] well" (3:4; see also 3:12). A measure of sound teaching was the degree to which it inspired and enabled people to live in ways that reflected "God's way of doing things" (1 Tim 1:4) that is God's ordering of the "house" of creation or God's managing of the economy of salvation.

"The goal of instruction is love from a pure heart, a good conscience, and a sincere faith" (1:5), Paul writes. In Galatians, Paul wrote that the "fruit of the Spirit" is, first and primarily, "love" (Gal 5:22). Here he says the overarching purpose of teaching is to produce love. He affirms that there are three enduring virtues—faith, hope, and love—and that "the greatest of these is love" (1 Cor 13:13). Of course, Paul was echoing Jesus, who insisted that love for God and love for neighbor were the aim of the Hebrew Scriptures. He also gave a "new commandment" to love one another as he had loved them. This was the clearest witness his followers could give (John 13:34-35).

It is not enough for teaching to impart information, as vital as information surely is, and it's not sufficient for teaching to increase knowledge, though knowledge is surely necessary. Authentic Christian teaching helps transform self-centeredness into empathy and compassion for others. It enlarges our capacity for love.

Love rises from a "pure heart" (1:5), the kind of heart for which the psalmist prayed: "Create a clean heart for me, God; put a new, faithful spirit deep inside me!" (Ps 51:10). A pure heart is not cluttered with accumulated guilt and clogged with knotted resentments. Instead, it flows with forgiveness freely received and freely given.

Love has the support of a "good conscience" (1:5), which discerns, on the basis of intuition trained by experience, between right and wrong, healthy and unhealthy, and good and evil. Many Jewish thinkers had borrowed and expanded the idea of "good conscience" from Greek philosophers. Those philosophers believed that the Creator had implanted in the mind and heart of each person a capacity for recognizing and learning morality by observing the consequences of behavior.

Love is also the companion of "sincere faith" (1:5)—of trust that God's ordering of the world is for human flourishing and for the wholeness of creation. "Sincere" faith is not the same thing as "simple" faith, however. Faith can be complex and difficult. "Sincere" faith isn't necessarily easy, but it is authentic, honest, and transparent. Active and compassionate love is the main outward expression of this faith, reflecting an inner settled and centered confidence in God's grace and mercy.

The wrong teaching Paul told Timothy to confront "missed this goal" (1:6). Because love was no longer the central purpose of these misleading teachers, they had been "distracted by talk that doesn't mean anything" (1:6). These distracted teachers wanted to be "teachers of Law without understanding either what they [were] saying or what they [were] talking about with such confidence" (1:7). Talking confidently without understanding is a characteristic of teachers who mislead others. Often such false teachers are charismatic, well-polished, and self-assured. They sound convincing because they appear convinced. The contents of their message can be false, but it can seem true because the packaging is so attractive and appealing.

Apparently, these distracted teachers cited the law of Moses to bolster their claims of truthfulness. The law in itself was not the problem. Paul himself said, "the Law is good if used appropriately" (1:8). Rather, the problem was the teachers' mishandling of the law. According to Paul, an appropriate use of the law is to provide moral authority for people who lack it from a better source, such as the teaching he urged Timothy to provide.

Remember that Timothy had been tutored by Paul, who was steeped in the Jewish faith. Timothy's teaching would have made use of the Torah in ways that faithfully reflected Jesus' and Paul's understanding of it as a testimony of Israel's covenant relationship with their liberating God. Paul wasn't tossing out the law, but he recognized that it could be a dangerous weapon in the hands of distracted teachers who cared more about esoteric secrets that they supposedly unearthed from it than they cared for the Bible's witness to the steadfast love of God.

These harmful teachers, who didn't know or remember that love is the goal of all healthy instruction, are confirmation of the importance of 1 Timothy. Letters like this remind those who lead Christian communities that love—Jesus' kind of love—is what church is all about.

Notes

Notes

2

BLAMELESS
CHARACTER

1 Timothy 3: 1-13

Central Question

What makes a good Christian leader?

Scripture

1 Timothy 3:1-13

1 This saying is reliable: if anyone has a goal to be a supervisor in the church, they want a good thing. 2 So the church's supervisor must be without fault. They should be faithful to their spouse, sober, modest, and honest. They should show hospitality and be skilled at teaching. 3 They shouldn't be addicted to alcohol or a bully. Instead, they should be gentle, peaceable, and not greedy. 4 They should manage their own household well—they should see that their children are obedient with complete respect, 5 because if they don't know how to manage their own household, how can they take care of God's church? 6 They shouldn't be new believers so that they won't become proud and fall under the devil's spell. 7 They should also have a good reputation with those outside the church so that they won't be embarrassed and fall into the devil's trap. 8 In the same way, servants in the church should be dignified, not two-faced, heavy drinkers, or greedy for money. 9 They should hold on to the faith that has been revealed with a clear conscience. 10 They should also be tested and then serve if they are without fault. 11 In the same way, women who are servants in the church should be dignified and not gossip. They should be sober and faithful in everything they do. 12 Servants must be faithful to their spouse and manage their

children and their own households well. 13 Those who have served well gain a good standing and considerable confidence in the faith that is in Christ Jesus.

Reflecting

During watercooler chat at the office one day, a coworker casually mentioned he and his wife were looking forward to watching the NFL draft that week. I did a double take. It's not often that husbands and wives who are not apparent sports fans spend any time, much less three days, watching a process so arcane and overhyped that BBC coverage of the international chess championship seems accessible by comparison. I delved a little deeper.

"I am a huge football fan," I said, "but even I don't watch the draft. What's the deal?"

He answered, "We just really like the drama of it. Seeing which teams take which players. It's cool to see the business side of the game played out in front of you."

My coworker wasn't alone. The 2014 draft had the largest viewing audience ever with more than 45.7 million people tuning in to watch the coverage on ESPN and ESPN2 (Bibel). That was a 28 percent increase over the previous year.

What explains this phenomenon? It can be partly explained by Americans' interest in professional football and their own team's strategy in selecting players. There's also something deeper involved. We all like to think we can evaluate talent. We like to pretend we are the general manager, predicting who will perform the best on the field. It's the same motivation behind the growing participation in fantasy football, in which people draft teams of real players, receiving points each week for their "pretend" team by compiling the performances of their players.

Today's text reveals the Apostle Paul's criteria for selecting church leaders. It's an important list for Timothy to convey to the church at Ephesus because choosing good leaders is essential for a church's success. How do the qualities in 1 Timothy 3 match up with how you evaluate those who seek to serve the church? To what extent are these qualities apparent in your own character?

Studying

Last week, we explored sound faith. This week, it's sound leadership. Knowing what to look for in a minister or lay leader in the church can be difficult. If Scripture isn't our guide, poor choices can lead to division and strife.

To understand today's text, it's important to understand the leadership roles addressed. The first role mentioned is "supervisor" (v. 2). The literal English translation of the word from Greek is "overseer," though it has been traditionally translated as "bishop." The word appears throughout Scripture. Greek translations of the Old Testament use the term for military commanders in Judges and 2 Kings. It refers to managers in Numbers and Isaiah, and it is even used to describe God in the book of Job. In the New Testament, it is used to describe Christ as well as early church leaders (Jefford, 116).

What exactly were a bishop's or supervisor's duties in the early church? The pastoral epistles outline a specific, formal position for the overseer. It is implied that there was one per congregation and that the overseer was charged with instruction of the believers, administration of ceremonial practices, and protection and preservation of Christian doctrine (Jefford, 116). The overseer also had duties related to economic management, hospitality, care of the poor and marginalized, and general arbitration of disputes within the community (Jefford, 116). Although modern-day bishops provide oversight for all the congregations within a given region, the supervisors described in 1 Timothy provided oversight within a single congregation.

Who can be a supervisor in the church? Stated generally, this must be someone who practices what they preach. Their lives must reflect what the church is all about (Wright, 28). They must model the gospel message. They should live out their humanity with enough of a distinction from the culture around them that they can speak to the culture with moral objectivity. The specific requirements are straightforward: be without fault, faithful to one's spouse, sober, modest, honest, hospitable, an effective teacher, not addicted to alcohol, not a bully, gentle, peaceable, not greedy, a good home-manager and parent, not a new believer, and have a good reputation outside of the church. Simple, right?

The list does not include "must be a male." The Common English Bible does not use masculine language in this text. Greek grammar calls for masculine forms when referring to mixed-gender groups (Wright, 29). This has led many translations to emphasize "maleness" in these descriptions. And it was indeed likely that most if not all supervisors were male in the early days of Christianity because the Roman world was a male-dominated society. By not differentiating between male and female, however, the CEB holds to a more literal translation without reflecting this ancient cultural bias.

The phrase "faithful to their spouse" (v. 2) is sometimes translated "husband of one wife" (KJV, ESV). Though sometimes understood as a prohibition of divorced church leaders, this phrase most likely refers to polygamy, a common practice at that time (Wright, 30). Thus the New Revised Standard Version translates it "married only once." When understood in this light, the qualifications also do not exclude the service of single people.

The next list of qualifications has to do with "servants" (vv. 8, 10, 12), a word commonly translated as "deacons." This word is used thirty times in the New Testament in a variety of contexts. John's Gospel uses the term to refer to table waiters while in Matthew it is used to describe the servants of a king (Crockett, 200). The vast majority of references to the word "servant" are in the letters of Paul. As an official position within the church, "servants" are mentioned in Philippians 1 as well as Romans 16, where Paul specifically mentions a servant or deacon named Phoebe. (Verse 11 speaks simply of "women," which could refer to "female deacons" as easily as to "wives of deacons" as in the KJV.)

The role of the deacon in many churches has largely been administrative, but the servants in the early church were more engaged in benevolence ministry or pastoral care. They looked after the widows and orphans, freeing others to conduct ministries of evangelism and proclamation.

As with supervisors, our passage enumerates a list of character traits rather than skills or accomplishments necessary for holding the office of servant. The list is similar to that of the supervisor: dignified, not two-faced, not a heavy drinker, not greedy, and that they should hold on to the faith. Qualifications are then enumerated for women servants of the church: dignified, not gossipers, and faithful in everything. The list continues with admonitions that would apply equally to both genders: faithful to their spouses and managing their children and households well. As with supervisors, this list of character traits does not exclude women—indeed, it specifically includes them in verse 11—and there is no mention of anything that could be mistaken for a prohibition of divorced persons serving.

The most important point about these two lists is that they describe character traits, not skills. Paul is not a human resources executive telling Timothy who should be hired. Rather, these lists speak to a person's character and help focus the decision-making process for leadership on how much a person emulates Christ and lives apart from the worldly culture.

Understanding

Perhaps this text has been controversial in your church's life and challenging in your own faith journey. Instead of highlighting character traits needed for church leadership, this passage has often been used to exclude people from service. Whether it's women or those who have gone through a divorce, these lists have been twisted to create disunity within a church. They are often quoted when debates over who is qualified for service arise.

Which of these many character traits seems most important in your church's ministry context? Why?

Later culturally-bound interpretations of this passage have been given much more weight than the direct meaning of Paul's instructions. By focusing on these secondary issues, the church has often missed the point of the character requirements. It can be much easier on our consciences to look at this text and pick out the supposed exclusions based on gender or marital status. It's much trickier to go down the list of character traits and seek God's direction in selecting a leader.

Because the first trait listed is to be "without fault" (v. 10), we might be tempted to read this list as an unattainable ideal. Reminiscent of the words of Jesus in the Beatitudes (Matt 5:3-11), these qualifications can feel beyond our grasp. They can leave us wondering who *really* is qualified to serve? It's important to look at this list as a target at which to aim rather than a checklist to which we must completely adhere. Churches have enough trouble finding sound leaders without subjecting every potential candidate to a standard of perfection that the bulk of the congregation is unwilling to follow themselves!

This raises the question: Who should live by these standards? Are they meant only for those who want to serve? Like the fruit of the Spirit (Gal 5:22-23), these qualifications can help us understand what a Christian's life should look like—particularly to those outside of the church.

What About Me?

• *Choose based on character.* Fall is often when churches make their selections for elected offices. As you consider who might be nominated, start with these lists. Pray over your decision and evaluate each candidate's potential to serve based on character, and not merely skills or past record of service.

• *Hold yourself to the same standard.* When applying these criteria to others, don't fall into the judgmental trap of excluding yourself from these lofty traits. Don't lose sight of your responsibility to live out the gospel in such a way that the outside world notices the difference and sees Christ in you.

• *Reconsider exclusion.* If you have always been taught that certain people are forbidden from service because of gender or marital status, pray for the Holy Spirit's direction in understanding this passage. Scripture can only transform us to the extent that we are open to hearing it with humility, acknowledging we still have more to learn. Whatever we conclude, we honor God when we sacrifice our preconceptions and allow God's word to speak.

• *Be open to service.* God has a way of calling on the unexpected to fulfill vital roles of ministry. If you have never thought of yourself as a church leader, be open to the possibility that God may want to use you in such a role. Or, if your sincere spiritual discernment has confirmed that a formal church office is not for you, ask God to show you how else you can best serve the body of Christ.

Resources

Sara Bibel, "Record 45.7 Million Viewers for 2014 NFL Draft" *TVbytheNumbers.com*, 12 May 2014 <http://tvbythenumbers.zap2it.com/2014/05/12/record-45-7-million-viewers-for-2014-nfl-draft/263063/>.

Bennie R. Crockett, "Deacon," *Mercer Dictionary of the Bible*, ed. Watson E. Mills et al. (Macon GA: Mercer University Press, 1990).

Clayton N. Jefford, "Bishop," *Mercer Dictionary of the Bible*, ed. Watson E. Mills et al. (Macon GA: Mercer University Press, 1990).

N. T. Wright, *Paul for Everyone: The Pastoral Letters* (Louisville KY: Westminster John Knox, 2003).

BLAMELESS CHARACTER

1 Timothy 3: 1-13

Who Is a Leader?

The word "leader" conjures up in my mind quite a crowded room of people, many of whom are so different from each other that they wouldn't necessarily have been very comfortable had I put them together. Sojourner Truth, former slave and tireless crusader for the abolition of slavery and for women's rights, is there, ready to recite "Ain't a Woman?" to whomever is willing to listen—as well as to people who aren't willing at all. Marlene Holland, my junior high school social studies teacher is there because she encouraged me at a time when I desperately needed someone to believe in my potential.

Mohandas Gandhi and Martin Luther King, Jr., are there, deeply engaged in conversation about the power of nonviolent resistance to effect social change. A few business leaders are there: Lee Iacocca, one of Detroit's great car guys; Steve Jobs, founder of Apple Computers and an extraordinary designer and marketer; and Max De Pree, retired chairman and CEO of the Herman Miller Company, who learned from Jesus about leading as a servant. Robert Shaw, legendary choral and symphonic conductor, is there. Some great coaches are there: Dean Smith, Vince Lombardi, and Bobby Dodd.

Ken Haag, my boyhood pastor, who profoundly shaped my understanding of ministry, is there. So are two pastors I only know through their writings: Harry Emerson Fosdick and Carlyle Marney. There are many laymen and laywomen from the churches I have been honored to serve. When I think of leader-ship, these faces, among others, come to mind, because they inspired and motivated people to be and do more than they would otherwise have been and done.

Often, we're ambivalent about leadership. We need it and resist it, clamor for it and criticize it, depend on it and sabotage it. Our ambivalence is rooted in our anxiety about change, which leaders inevitably challenge us to make, and in our wariness about power, which leaders exercise and too frequently abuse. Our ambivalence is understandable, and it's also crucial for us to manage it constructively, so that we may have healthy and effective leaders for our communities, businesses, governments, nonprofits, and churches.

New Testament Views of Leadership

Our churches need good leaders. As today's text underscores, goodness includes both blameless character ("without fault," v. 2) and competence (able to "take care of God's church," v. 5). Very early in the church's history, it became clear that some people were gifted in, and experienced an inward call to, serving the Christian community by providing an example of Christlikeness, helping other followers of Jesus to grow, and enhancing the community's ability to fulfill its mission.

The New Testament doesn't give us a straightforward description of how we should organize our churches, the titles we should give our leaders, or the specific "job responsibilities" those leaders should fulfill. Instead, what the Scriptures offer us are sketches of a variety of diverse churches that, like our churches, had a variety of structures—some fluid and changing, others more established and settled. The Bible also describes an array of leadership roles and functions, some informal and others more formal. For these reasons, we can't appeal to the New Testament in support of any particular organizational structure or position of leadership.

Most of the churches we glimpse in the New Testament had what we would call a pastor, someone whose role was to "shepherd the flock"—to tend to its health, to nurture its faithfulness, and to care for its members. A pastor was sometimes called bishop ("supervisor" or "overseer"). At other times, pastors were called "elders," connoting wisdom born of experience more than age.

Often, the person we would consider the lead or senior pastor was the central leader within a collegial group of other leaders. In that collegial group, or in close partnership with it, there were also deacons (literally, "servants"). It also seems likely that, in some regions, there were "pastors of pastors," a role for which the term bishop expanded to include responsibility for the oversight of a fellowship of churches.

We're not certain about which of these leaders were ordained. In fact, ordination as a formal designation emerged slowly and unevenly in the church. The practice of ordination, though, has its roots in the ways early churches designated, commissioned, and blessed their most accountable leaders, often with the laying on of hands (see Acts 6:1-6; 1 Tim 4:14; 5:22; 2 Tim 1:6).

First Timothy 3:1-13 describes the qualities the early church sought in its "supervisors" (CEB) or "bishops" (NRSV). This role was roughly equivalent to what we most often call a "pastor." The passage also indicates the expectations the church had for its "servants" (CEB) or "deacons" (NRSV). "Supervisors" needed to demonstrate steady and loving commitment to their families: "faithful to their spouse" (v. 2) and able to "manage their own household well" (v. 4). The church looked for similar marks of domestic stability and affection in its "servants" (see v. 12).

The phrase that the Common English Bible translates "faithful to their spouse" is translated "married only once" in the New Revised Standard Version (v. 2). A more literal translation is "the husband of one wife." While it's doubtless true that the vast majority of supervisors or bishops in the early church were male, I don't think the phrase "husband of one wife" can legitimately be used to bolster the case that pastors must be men. Later in this passage, when discussing the qualifications of "servants," Paul refers to the women who served in that role (v. 11). The word translated "women" there can be rendered "wives," but there is a more specific Greek word for wives than Paul used. It's most likely that Paul was referring to women who were "servants" or "deacons" (see Rom 16:1). There were contexts and circumstances in which Paul restricted the role of women in a particular church (see, for instance, in this same epistle, the vexing and difficult-to-interpret words of 2:11-15).

Paul's concern, evidently, was to protect the church's reputation in the wider culture where, in some places, female leadership of a religious group was suspect. That same principle—not to embarrass the church by virtue of who is allowed to lead it—would, in our time, argue for the full inclusion of women in every leadership role rather than for any kind of exclusion. Such full inclusion would also express Paul at his best, such as in Galatians, where he gave voice to the radical and full equality that should characterize the church: "There is neither Jew nor Greek; there is neither slave nor free; nor is there male and female, for you are all one in Christ Jesus" (Gal 3:28).

Nor do I think that the phrase communicates the expectation that pastors must be married. After all, Jesus himself was single! I think the phrase most straightforwardly forbids its leaders from the widespread practice of polygamy.

In my view, these texts about family life don't have a significant contribution to make to contemporary debates about whether or not divorced persons can be pastors or deacons. Everyone who has experienced or seriously considered divorce knows its causes are most often tragic and tangled with failure, heartache, sin, and regret. It's heartrending when anyone's marriage fails. God's mercy is for those who experience the brokenness of divorce, just as it is for those who endure every other kind of brokenness. Grace extends to those whose relationships fail.

Mercy and grace don't allow us to take divorce lightly, but they do permit us to consider the possibility that it doesn't permanently disqualify people who demonstrate that they have learned from, and have even been transformed by, their painful experiences. I don't think there's a simple and single rule. In every instance, it's a matter for prayerful and careful discernment.

The early church expected that its supervisors would "manage their...household[s] well" and that their children would be "obedient with complete respect" (v. 4). They also expected that servants would "manage their children and their own households well" (v. 12). Last week, we noted that the first-century church, influenced by its culture, made a connection between God's ways of managing the house of creation and human leadership of other "houses"—communities of various kinds, villages, towns, and cities, and the nation itself. This view of leadership as household management came, of course, from the original household, which was the extended family.

It's understandable, then, that the early church thought that leaders' ways of shaping and guiding their family life would indicate how those leaders would function in a church family. If leaders created unhealthy conflict and generated continual chaos in their families, it was likely they would cause the same kind of harm to the church. So, Paul asked, "If they don't know how to manage their own household, how can they take care of God's church?" (v. 5).

We shouldn't expect perfection, however, from imperfect people, and we are all imperfect. Leaders' children can and sometimes do rebel against even the wisest and most loving parents. Many families, including the families of pastors and deacons, endure seasons of difficulty. The issue for us, I think, is how those leaders respond to such challenges. Do they manifest the spirit of Jesus, who, after all, told the parable of the prodigal son and used the father of a wayward child as an image of God?

Inner Life, Outer Witness

In the early church, which lived amid misunderstanding and even persecution, there was a great concern that nothing in their leaders' conduct would give hostile forces reason to disparage the community of faith. In the eyes of outsiders, disorderly family life was one possible source of embarrassment for the church. So were falling to the temptations of pride (v. 6), greedily mishandling their own or the church's money (vv. 3, 8), and being addicted to alcohol (vv. 3, 8). The church needed—and needs—for its leaders to "have a good reputation with those outside" (v. 7).

For the sake of both the church's inner life and its outer witness, its leaders must be "sober, modest, and honest" (v. 2), "gentle, peaceable, and not greedy" (v. 3), "not two-faced" (v. 8), "dignified and not gossip[s].... and faithful in everything they do" (v.11). The need for such demonstrated character explains why these leaders "shouldn't be new believers" (v. 6). They were to be "tested and then serve if they are without fault" (v. 10).

The supervisors were to "show hospitality" and to be "skilled at teaching" (v. 2). The ability to teach is central to the work of a supervisor or pastor. The church depends for its essential identity and effectiveness on regular engagement with the living Word of God to which the written words of Scripture bear witness.

Hospitality—welcoming strangers and providing shelter and food for travelers—was a common expectation of people shaped by the Hebrew Scriptures and by the example of Jesus. Here, since the phrase is linked with the ability to teach, Paul likely meant that the supervisors would gladly welcome traveling missionaries and teachers (such as himself) into their homes.

The church expected its servants or deacons to "hold on to the faith that [had] been revealed with a clear conscience" (v. 9). Certainly, the church had the same expectation for all its members. Paul underscored this qualification for the role of servant because otherwise it would be too easy to reduce it to the carrying out of mundane and practical tasks. It's important to remember that the early church's first deacons were organizers and hosts of community meals and food distribution (see Acts 6:1-7). Paul emphasized that there are sacred dimensions to such simple deeds. Feeding the hungry is an act of compassion that reflects the will and way of Jesus. It's a witness to faith in him (v. 13).

Such bearing witness to Jesus—reflecting his character and commitments—is a leader's job and the church's mission.

Notes

Notes

3

INSPRING

EXAMPLE

1 Timothy 4: 7b-16

Central Question

For whom do I set an example?

Scripture

1 Timothy 4:7b-16

7 Train yourself for a holy life! 8 While physical training has some value, training in holy living is useful for everything. It has promise for this life now and the life to come. 9 This saying is reliable and deserves complete acceptance. 10 We work and struggle for this: "Our hope is set on the living God, who is the savior of all people, especially those who believe." 11 Command these things. Teach them. 12 Don't let anyone look down on you because you are young. Instead, set an example for the believers through your speech, behavior, love, faith, and by being sexually pure. 13 Until I arrive, pay attention to public reading, preaching, and teaching. 14 Don't neglect the spiritual gift in you that was given through prophecy when the elders laid hands on you. 15 Practice these things, and live by them so that your progress will be visible to all. 16 Focus on working on your own development and on what you teach. If you do this, you will save yourself and those who hear you.

Reflecting

At the age of twenty-two, I was asked to participate in a new pilot project of Big Brothers, Big Sisters in a local elementary school.

Rather than the usual full-time commitment, this experimental project enlisted mentors who met with kids at school for an hour each week.

As a single man with no children, I was intimidated by the prospect of interacting with a child. The day I was introduced to my new "little brother," an anxiety I hadn't felt before swept over me. I signed in, and the school counselor escorted me to a small windowed conference room in the library. They brought in my new little brother, a well-mannered and smiling first grader who politely shook my hand and stared at me. When the counselor left, my little brother began to fidget. Soon, he was crawling under the table, on top of the table, pulling books off the shelves lining the room, and literally running circles around me. After an hour, I was exhausted, my new little brother went back to class, and I was convinced that the entire experience did not help anyone.

We met together for three years, and my little brother's behavior slowly improved. We had meaningful conversations. I learned he had a twin who was physically disabled and used a motorized wheelchair. I learned that although he knew his father, his father wasn't in the picture, and that his mother worked long hours to support him and his brother and their older sister, who babysat them most of the time.

I saw his reading improve as we read together. I witnessed his behavior improve as he began taking medication for attention deficit disorder. I participated in his blossoming relationships with classmates as we ate lunches together in the school cafeteria. By the time the program ended, I felt I had made a difference and that it had been a profoundly mutual experience in which we both had grown. Even when it's a formal relationship, serving as a role model changes you and the people around you.

Studying

We expect our church leaders to serve as role models. We read passages like today's text and say, "Yes, *those* people should exhibit godly character." We are more reluctant to embrace such standards for ourselves, however. But what's good for the pastor is good for the people. After all, it's not just the pastor who stands as a role model.

Paul compares the Christian life to physical activity. It's similar to 1 Corinthians 9, in which the Apostle uses the imagery of running a race and being disciplined like a boxer (Wright, 46).

This exhortation sounds remarkably contemporary. We are familiar with working out in our fitness-obsessed twenty-first century. Surfing the channels early in the morning reveals dozens of commercials for workout products and plans to help us get in shape. With names like "Extreme" and "Insanity," the not-so-subtle implications of these products and programs are that these exercise regimens require work. This is also the point Paul is making about training for holy living. Our spiritual life is more than experiencing "a sense of the presence of God" (Wright, 46). We are to actively engage in spiritual disciplines Paul describes as "work and struggle" (v. 10). He also promises benefits both here and now and in the life to come.

We receive power to help us in this work, however. Paul writes, "Our hope is set on the living God, who is the savior of all people" (v. 10). How one understands the meaning of the phrase "savior of all people" is a function of emphasis. There are at least three possible interpretations:

(1) Everyone will be saved, but those who believe in the gospel will enjoy a relationship with God in the present.
(2) God is the potential savior for everyone if they believe. There is no other savior.
(3) This God through this Jesus is the true savior, through which the entire world will be rescued from decay and injustice, but because humans retain the right to refuse God's offer, only believers will find salvation (Wright, 48).

The conclusion of this section is action-oriented. Pay attention to the verbs Paul uses: "command" (v. 11), "teach" (v. 11), "don't let anyone look down on you" (v. 12), "set an example" (v. 12). Here is the heart of Paul's pastoral advice. Paul challenges Timothy to lead and not merely be present with the congregation. Those who have endured authoritarian relationships may shy from such seemingly heavy-handed admonitions as "command," but in Paul's day, the church was so new it had to have clear and strong direction.

As noted in a previous lesson, there were false teachers in Ephesus. A strong word was needed to counteract their influence. The gospel will be undermined if Timothy acts timidly because he is young. Paul says age is not a qualification for authority in this case. Timothy must preach and teach the truth and trust God to back it up (Wright, 51).

Although Timothy's youth shouldn't undermine his ministry, neither should his character. Paul gives Timothy a clear formula to follow: speech, behavior, love, faith, and sexual purity (v. 12). Each of these aspects of character had the potential to disrupt Timothy's ministry and send the church into chaos and confusion. This is equally true today—for both the clergy and the laity.

There are only two ways to determine a person's character: through what they do and what they say. Paul addresses both. It was important in the first century for followers of this new religion to show good moral character to build a good reputation among outsiders. How much more important is it today, when the world knows the basics of Christian teaching and yet sees very few examples of genuine Christlikeness! Unfortunately, the oft-cited quote from British writer G. K. Chesterton is all too true: "The Christian ideal has not been tried and found wanting. It has been found difficult; and left untried" (Chesterton, 48).

To keep in check the legalistic tendencies of his audience (see 1:7-9; 4:3-4), Paul adds mention of "love" and "faith" (v. 12). These qualities temper our pursuit of high moral character. We must not lose sight of love for God and fellow humans. Nor must we attempt to follow a rigid moral code without accepting by faith that the God who calls us to live such a life can empower us to do so.

The admonition to remain sexually pure would no doubt set Timothy apart from the culture of Ephesus. Ephesus was a port city and thus home to all the activities a cosmopolitan port city promoted (Blevins, 256). By not following the sexual mores of the culture, Christians distinguished themselves even more clearly than by generally following rules and being nice.

This aspect of today's text is also eerily applicable today. Christians have been public in their denunciation of sexual sin even as our culture glories in these excesses. It seems less appealing to Christians, however, to scrutinize their own lives and address their own shortcomings.

Finally, Paul concludes with instructions on self-care, explicitly stating Timothy should work on his "own development" (v. 16). Exhibiting good moral character and teaching God's truth cannot be achieved without cultivating God's gifts in ourselves (Wright, 52). It's important to dedicate time to focusing on our growth. It's not selfish to follow the model of Christ and make time to be present with God.

Understanding

This passage calls Christians—especially Christian leaders— to serve as role models for others. But how can we do this without flaunting our morality and religiosity? In Matthew 6, Jesus warned his followers to "be careful that you don't practice your religion in front of people to draw their attention. If you do, you will have no reward from your Father who is in heaven" (Matt 6:1).

There is a difference, however, between drawing attention to ourselves as role models and exhibiting Christian character in such a way that others will be inspired to live better. After all, Jesus also said, "Let your light shine before people, so they can see the good things you do and praise your Father who is in heaven" (Matt 5:16).

Seventeenth-century philosopher John Selden wrote about hypocrisy in his book *Table Talk*, "Preachers say, 'Do as I say, not as I do'" (see "Do as I say"). This is at the heart of today's text. What does it mean to claim to follow Christ if we don't strive to match our profession of faith to our behavior. We must be different from the culture around us in tangible and visible ways. All too often, however, we try to blend in so that those around us discern no difference in us. We call it "identifying with the culture" when really, more often than not, it is compromise.

Paul doesn't let anyone off the hook. He knows Christlikeness is difficult, but he invites us to embrace this struggle. We can't read this passage without giving serious thought to how we are leading our lives and whether we can distinguish our behavior from that of the culture around us.

What About Me?

• *Training is work.* The problem with applying this text to our lives isn't that we don't understand what we are supposed to do. The problem is, are we willing? If we can grasp what is involved with merely physical training, we understand the dedication that is required of followers of Christ.

> Who has been a role model for you in your career? As a parent? As a Christian?

• *Hope is our fuel.* It's easy to become frustrated with failure as we strive to set a proper example for others. By putting our hope in God, we can draw motivation and comfort that God is our savior and will be present with us in our training.

• *Word and deed.* Be consistent with what you say and what you do. Don't ignore the nudging of the Holy Spirit when you contemplate a course of action—or are confronted with the consequences of past actions. Our speech should match our behavior because actions speak louder than words.

• *Set an example.* A Scripture text like this is a clear call to living differently. Examine your life, let the Scripture speak to you, and embrace these words as a call to exhibit godly character. Without calling attention to yourself, let you lifestyle speak for itself.

Resources

James L. Blevins, "Ephesus," *Mercer Dictionary of the Bible*, ed. Watson E. Mills et al. (Macon GA: Mercer University Press, 1990).

G. K. Chesterton, *What's Wrong with the World* (New York: Dodd, Mead & Company, 1912).

"Do as I say," *The American Heritage Dictionary of Idioms*, <http://dictionary.reference.com/browse/do as i say>.

N. T. Wright, *Paul for Everyone: The Pastoral Letters* (Louisville KY: Westminster John Knox, 2003).

INSPRING

EXAMPLE

1 Timothy 4: 7b-16

Images of Jesus

For a long time, it has intrigued me that the New Testament nowhere describes Jesus' physical appearance. It gives us no clues about whether he was short or tall, stocky or lanky, or had a full or scraggly beard.

I think the absence of such physical description is a gift to us, because it allows our images of Jesus to come from the faces of men and women who remind us of him. Jesus looks like Mother Teresa, who cradled the dying poor of Calcutta in her arms, or like the teacher who pours her life's energy into drawing autistic children into meaningful community, or like Dietrich Bonhoeffer, who was executed in a Nazi prison camp because he refused to renounce his faith and yield to Hitler, or like the man who patiently taught your Sunday School class when you were a child. These flesh-and-blood images of Jesus could be people who risked their lives in daring acts of courage. They could also be people who gave their lives away over time in small but no-less-brave ways. They are models for us of what it is like to live a Jesus kind of life. Their examples encourage us to be like him. They make goodness attractive, holiness intriguing, and commitment compelling.

The Apostle Paul wanted Timothy, his younger partner in ministry, to be that kind of example for the church in Ephesus. He wrote, "Set an example for the believers through your speech, behavior, love, faith, and by being sexually pure" (1 Tim 4:12). Timothy's ways of speaking and living, his commitment to grow in the virtues of love and faith, and his honorable and respectful relationships with others were to reflect the spirit and teachings of Jesus.

Legendary actor-dancer Fred Astaire once said, "The hardest job kids face today is learning good manners without seeing any." It's a commonsense but often overlooked observation, not just about kids but also about all of us: we need examples of the kind of life we hope to live. Like Timothy, church leaders—indeed, all followers of Jesus—have the opportunity and responsibility to set that kind of example.

Being an Example

Evidently, Paul was concerned that Timothy might be reluctant to offer the church the gift of his example (and the gifts of his ministry) because of his comparative youthfulness. Paul urges him, "Don't let anyone look down on you because you are young" (4:12). As we'll see in next week's lesson, Paul felt the need to offer guidance for Timothy's relationships with older church members (5:1-2).

We're not sure whether Timothy faced criticism because of his age and relative lack of ministry experience, or if Timothy felt an internal lack of confidence, or both. Whatever the case, Paul reminded Timothy that the church in Ephesus needed for him to share the abilities and talents which God had given him and which the elders had affirmed in him. "Don't neglect the spiritual gift in you that was given through prophecy when the elders laid hands on you" (4:14), he writes. In the act of blessing or ordaining Timothy, at least some of the older people in the church had already expressed their confidence in his capacity for leadership. He didn't need to hesitate to lead.

When I was young in both years and experience, the good people of the Rocky Ford Baptist Church in Rocky Ford, Georgia, asked me to serve as their interim pastor. I was a student at nearby Georgia Southern College (now University) and, since I didn't really know what I didn't know about ministry, I agreed.

I had been there for about a month when the chair of deacons told me that, on the next Sunday evening, we'd be having a baptism and sharing the Lord's Supper. It wasn't a big deal to him. After all, for years they'd been observing what they called "the ordinances" on fifth-Sunday nights. He said, "It will be a kind of a night off for you. You'll just need to lead us in prayer, read a little Scripture, do the baptizing, and call us to the Table." I smiled as if I thought what we'd do the next Sunday night was as routine as he said. Inside, I was in a mild panic. I'd never performed a baptism and never presided at the Table.

All week long I fretted, but when the time for "the ordinances" came, I managed to baptize two of the church's children and lead the church in the experience of Communion. Here's how I got through the evening: the deacons of the church, who sensed my nervousness, coached me about what to do, and I did exactly what I remembered Ken Haag, my boyhood pastor, had done when he baptized and presided at the Table. I said what he said, quoted the Scripture he quoted, stood like he stood, moved like he moved, and gestured like he gestured. These "elders"—the deacons of the Rocky Ford Church as well as my former pastor—encouraged me.

Likewise, Paul offered his own encouragement to Timothy, and he also called to Timothy's mind the support he had received from other, and older, church leaders. Timothy's youthfulness was not a barrier to the effectiveness of his ministry.

Training for Holiness

Paul knew that for Timothy to be able to set the kind of example the Christians in Ephesus needed for him to set, the young minister would have to train. He urged Timothy, "Train yourself for a holy life" (4:7).

The necessity of training for holiness—of engaging in practices and disciplines that help us to become more like Jesus—is part of an unavoidable and creative tension in the spiritual life. On the one hand, salvation is a sheer gift of grace. On the other, it is a demand for our intentional cooperation with the transformation that grace intends to effect in us.

Paul wrote about this tension between gift and demand in Ephesians 2:8-10:

> You are saved by God's grace because of your faith. This salvation is God's gift. It's not something you possessed. It's not

something you did that you can be proud of. Instead, we are God's accomplishment, created in Christ Jesus to do good things. God planned for these good things to be the way that we live our lives.

The good things we do don't save us, but we are saved to do good things. And doing those good things requires effort on our part. The training in which Paul urged Timothy to engage is an example of such effort.

Attaining excellence in the arts, a profession, or a craft requires practice. We learn by doing. As we work devotedly and repeatedly at honing our abilities, we become more capable and more effective. I am an avid music lover, and my tastes run from classical to strange. I particularly like well-played guitar music in nearly any genre: classical, slide, blues, bluegrass, jazz, and rock and roll. When I was a teenager, I owned a guitar. When "Stairway to Heaven" or "Purple Haze" or "Freebird" was blaring from my stereo speakers, I would hold the guitar, strike a rocker's pose, and think to myself how cool it would be to play the guitar like those musicians played it. On my own, I picked up a few chords and could strum a decent church youth-group style chorus, but I never took a lesson and hardly ever practiced I owned a guitar. I admired great guitarists. I liked the idea of being able to play, but I was unwilling to practice—to train.

There are dimensions of Christian living that we develop in the same ways we learn a set of skills or hone a craft. We apprentice ourselves to people—and ultimately, of course, to Jesus—who show us how to see, hear, feel, think, and do as Jesus did. We learn how to pray, to forgive, to serve, to be compassionate, to be generous, and to be peacemakers by practicing these virtues. It takes time and effort to displace our egos from the center of our concerns and to allow love for God and others to permeate the details of how we lead our everyday lives. It requires discipline to respond to the challenges and opportunities as Jesus responded to his. We have to train.

Paul makes a comparison between spiritual and physical training, writing, "While physical training has some value, training in holy living is useful for everything. It has promise for this life now and the life to come" (1 Tim 4:8). The greater value of spiritual training seemed self-evident to him: "This saying is reliable and deserves complete acceptance" (4:9).

These verses echo the more extended comparison Paul elaborated in 1 Corinthians 9, where he borrowed imagery from the ancient Olympics. "Don't...all the runners in the stadium run, but only one gets the prize?" he writes. "So run to win" (1 Cor 9:24). Of course, Paul knew that winning a race depended on far more than merely entering it. It depends on rigorous training, so he added, "Everyone who competes practices self-discipline in everything" (9:25).

A runner in training gets up long before anyone else, even when she'd rather hit the snooze button. She laces up her running shoes and hits the road. A wrestler who's trying to reach or maintain his playing weight denies himself donuts and ice cream. A football player does time in the weight room four or five days a week. A golfer spends time out on the driving range. Basketball players practice free throws until they can shoot them with their eyes closed. Success in athletics requires discipline.

Paul also said to his Corinthian friends: athletes train "to get a crown of leaves that shrivel up and die, but we do it to receive a crown that never dies" (1 Cor 9:25). The garland wreath placed on the winning runner's head would soon wither.

Hanging in my garage is a red jacket with white leather sleeves. On those sleeves are gold numbers trimmed in red: 76. There's an old English "C" sewn on the left chest of the jacket and a snarling cougar on the right. It's my varsity football letter jacket, which I received in the fall of my sophomore year in high school, 1972. The leather sleeves are still in good shape, but all the other material has faded. The lining has worn thin, and the numbers are not as securely attached as they once were. That's how it goes: trophies tarnish, certificates fray, and newspaper clippings yellow. All these things are "perishable wreaths," which is why Paul told Timothy that even though physical training has some value, it's spiritual training that has greater and lasting value.

Paying Attention to the Work of Ministry

Not only did Paul want Timothy to train for holy living so
he could be a trustworthy example of Christlikeness to his
congregation, he also wanted him to attend diligently to the
routine but crucial aspects of ministry. "Pay attention to public
reading, preaching, and teaching" (4:13), he writes. It's likely that
"public reading" refers to the regular reading in public worship
of the Hebrew Scriptures, the emerging collections of accounts of
the words and deeds of Jesus (some of which became the Gospels
in the New Testament), and letters from respected leaders, such
as Paul. Preaching and teaching were central, then as now, to the
life of the church, since they helped followers of Jesus to weave
the good news of God's in-breaking kingdom into the fabric of
their lives.

In the final verse of today's passage, Paul summarizes what he
asked of Timothy: "Focus on working on your own development
and on what you teach. If you do this, you will save yourself
and those who hear you" (4:16). Paul called for a vital balance
between Timothy's personal and professional development,
between his private and public life, and between his identity as a
child of God and his role as a church leader. That kind of balance
is important for all Christians. We all have a responsibility to
find and maintain a healthy relationship between who we are and
what we do: between our personal and family lives on the one
hand and our work and community responsibilities on the other.
We must also find a balance between the nurture of our calling to
follow Jesus and the growth of our vocations and careers.

Notes

Notes

_____

_____

_____

_____

_____

_____

_____

_____

_____

_____

_____

_____

_____

_____

_____

_____

Proper
Relationships

1 Timothy 5: 1-7; 6: 1-2, 17-19

Central Question

Do I offer respect to all?

Scripture

1 Timothy 5:1-7; 6:1-2, 17-19

5:1 Don't correct an older man, but encourage him like he's your father; treat younger men like your brothers, 2 treat older women like your mother, and treat younger women like your sisters with appropriate respect. 3 Take care of widows who are truly needy. 4 But if a particular widow has children or grandchildren, they should first learn to respect their own family and repay their parents, because this pleases God. 5 A widow who is truly needy and all alone puts her hope in God and keeps on going with requests and prayers, night and day. 6 But a widow who tries to live a life of luxury is dead even while she is alive. 7 Teach these things so that the families will be without fault. 6:1 Those who are under the bondage of slavery should consider their own masters as worthy of full respect so that God's name and our teaching won't get a bad reputation. 2 And those who have masters who are believers shouldn't look down on them because they are brothers. Instead, they should serve them more faithfully, because the people who benefit from your good service are believers who are loved. Teach and encourage these things.... 17 Tell people who are rich at this time not to become egotistical and not to place their hope on their finances, which are uncertain. Instead, they need to hope in God, who richly provides everything for our enjoyment. 18 Tell them to do good, to be rich in the good things they do, to be generous, and to share with others. 19 When they do these things, they will save a treasure for themselves that is a good foundation for the future. That way they can take hold of what is truly life.

Reflecting

From 1996 to 2007, the now-defunct WB network aired a family drama called *7th Heaven*. This show followed the ups and downs of a pastor's family. The minister father and stay-at-home mother faced a range of issues that surfaced in their own lives, the lives of parishioners, and, of course, the lives of their seven children. By the time the series ended, however, the migration of actors to bigger and better opportunities changed the dynamics of the show. In order to stay true to the show's title, the writers kept the Camden house full of seven people (in addition to the parents) by having all manner of strays and hard-luck cases find their way into their lives.

The series tackled everything from premarital sex and cutting to caring for aging parents and interfaith dialogue. At times cheesy and at times poignant, *7th Heaven* portrayed a family that was vibrant and never, ever boring.

In his letter to Timothy, Paul instructs his protégé about how to relate to members of the congregation as if they were family members. The wisdom of responding to each member according to their age, sex, and social standing certainly had merit in Timothy's day. Even though our culture has dictated different roles and expectations today, this text has much to say to us about how to maintain proper relationships within the church.

> How has your family life prepared you to relate to others? What lessons might you need to "unlearn"?

As the *7th Heaven* theme song reminded viewers each week, "Where can you go when the world don't treat you right? The answer is home! That's the one place that you'll find seventh heaven." If there's anywhere you should be treated right, it's in the church, home to the family of faith.

Studying

Today's text comes from three different points in 1 Timothy 5–6. They are combined here because they share the common theme of relationship. Paul's pastoral advice in these passages is practical and relational. He tells Timothy how he should relate to various demographics within the church, including slaves and the wealthy. Despite the unique circumstances of that age and culture, this advice still holds up almost 2,000 years later for churches and pastors today.

Anyone who has ever had to confront a family member over a sensitive issue can relate to Paul's admonitions in chapter 5. The Apostle describes what Daniel Golman would call emotional intelligence. In the book by that name, Golman describes emotional intelligence as the ability to read one's own and other people's emotions and relate to others accordingly. It is inherently contextual. Paul understands that, as a pastor, you don't approach an older man the same way you would a younger woman. He spells out the best approaches based on the roles each fulfilled in the culture of that day.

Paul's advice is based on a traditional family model that would have been a familiar structure in the days of the early church much more so than now (Wright, 54). Paul repeats this metaphor in his letters to the church at Corinth, Ephesus, and Galatia, in which he refers to the "household of faith" (Knight, 291). Churches of the first century were more like an extended family than even small congregations are today. The members of the local congregation were often related, such as the family of Cornelius in Acts 10, or became family for each other because their conversion caused them to be cut off from their biological families. It's a safe bet that families in New Testament times had their share of dysfunction, but by using the family as a model for treating people in the church, Paul draws on a familiar set of guidelines.

Older men are to be treated with respect and gentleness, like one's father. Younger men are to be treated with love and mutual respect, like one's brother. Older women are to be treated like one's mother, the pillar of a family. And younger women are to be treated like sisters. Paul specifically cites the need to respect younger women. Since his culture was so male-dominated, Paul goes out of his way to instruct Timothy to respect younger women and not dismiss them. This is also a cautionary statement: if you have respect for younger women, you are less likely to objectify them and fall into sexual sin.

Life in New Testament times was particularly harsh for women who no longer had financial support from men. Throughout the New Testament, widows occupy a special place in God's providence and concern (Simmons, 959). Verses 3-6 provide specific instructions on their care. These verses indicate the church in Ephesus had a formal system involving widows as both receivers and givers of care (Simmons, 959). If a widow were younger, however, and had family to care for her or were likely to marry again (see v. 11), she was deemed not truly needy: other widows needed to be a higher priority for the church's limited resources (see v. 16). Furthermore, Paul pronounces a harsh judgment on widows who tried to "live a life of luxury" (v. 6), stating that such a one is "dead even while she is alive." Those who had enough to indulge themselves should not be receiving the church's aid.

Paul's even harsher condemnation, though, is for the family who does not take care of its widows (v. 8). A hallmark of Christian character is care and concern for others. If believers don't care even for the needy members of their own families, they are a terrible example to outsiders and a detriment to the church's reputation. It would also cause strife within the church if a widow had to be enrolled in the church benevolence program while her family ignored her needs.

Another tricky relationship to navigate in New Testament times was that of the slave owner and slave. Our modern sensibilities may lead us to resist this text. It's important to note, however, that just because Paul advises those participating in the institution of slavery how to live as Christians, he is not endorsing the owning of other human beings.

Slavery was part of the world in which Paul and Timothy ministered, but Paul suggests something completely antithetical to the culture: the slave owner and the slave are both equal before God and have equal standing in the church. We can't let the power dynamics of our culture influence how we relate to each other in the church. The wealthy are not to be catered to while the impoverished are ignored. There are too many examples of the privileged running churches—and ruining churches because they lose sight of God's calling and Christ's example, focusing instead on their own self-interest.

At the forefront of Paul's concern is believers' witness to the community, be they slave owners or slaves. In Paul's day, having an unbelieving master was not an excuse to be a disrespectful slave. Today, we might say that working for unbelievers is not an excuse to be a lousy employee. We have the ability to influence those in authority over us by the way we respond to them.

The final portion of the text selected for this lesson addresses the wealthy. For most American Christians, this means us. We are among the wealthiest people in the world, and we cannot let ourselves off the hook by comparing what we see as our own modest means compared to the wealthiest Americans. As part of the church, we are to be generous, not selfish, with our resources.

Understanding

There are no easy formulas for relationships, despite what you may read on the covers of magazines at the grocery store checkout line. Today's texts are not intended to serve as a substitute for real relationship. Paul isn't offering a checklist: Older man? Father figure. Older woman? Mother figure. Younger man or younger woman? Brother or sister. Slave owner? Respect. Wealthy? Be generous. Rather, he is providing wise counsel that can be generally helpful, but should not replace interacting with people on an individual basis.

If you reflect on your experience, you can easily come up with examples that go against Paul's advice. There are older men who respond to gentleness by taking advantage—yes, even in the church. There are older women who will not, for a variety of reasons, be able to show appreciation for the motherly respect you try to show them. And anyone with siblings knows the conflicting emotions of those relationships and just how painful they can be. Why would we want to transfer that onto our fellow believers? The people who hold power over us may not suddenly see things our way just because we show them more respect. That simply isn't the way relationships work in the real world.

Paul's advice to Timothy doesn't promise him a foolproof system. There are no foolproof systems when it comes to relationships, and we should be very suspicious when we encounter someone offering one. First Timothy is a letter from one pastor to another on how to be the best pastor possible. The best chance Timothy has to reach his congregation is with respect.

Repeatedly throughout this unit, we have made the connection between clergy and laity behaviors. It's no different here. If ministers can achieve the best relationships through respect, so can church members.

What About Me?

• *Your family is more than blood relations.* Whether you come from a large, tight-knit family with aunts and uncles and cousins and several generations still living or you have a very small family, you are part of a larger family when you are a part of a church. Don't be afraid to relate to church members as members of your family. Doing so is one of the most profound blessings of belonging to the body of Christ.

• *Relationships are contextual.* Everyone is different. There are no magic formulas for relationship success. With respect at the core, we must seek to understand the people around us if we want to successfully navigate life inside and outside the church. Relationships are unavoidable, and each person carries in them a unique glimpse of the face of God. Find out what that glimpse looks like and appreciate each person for who they are.

• *Widows are among you.* Too often we look past the forgotten members of our congregations because we fail to appreciate them for who they are. In the case of widows, particularly older women, our lives are enriched when we reach out and build relationships with them. Paul focuses on their financial and physical care, but the emotional needs of widows are just as real and just as important for the church to meet.

• *Respect and power.* When we struggle to live out our Christian convictions in an environment where we have no power, remember that we have an example. Christ was not politically, socially, or financially powerful. Even though he was provocative with religious authorities, he treated his wealthy followers the same as he did those who had little. He didn't punish them for having wealth, nor were they given special attention. That is a healthy model for the church.

Resources

Daniel Golman, *Emotional Intelligence: Why It Can Matter More Than IQ* (Bantam Books, 1995).

Douglas A. Knight, "Family," *Mercer Dictionary of the Bible*, ed. Watson E. Mills et al. (Macon GA: Mercer University Press, 1990).

Paul D. Simmons, "Widow in the New Testament," *Mercer Dictionary of the Bible*, ed. Watson E. Mills et al. (Macon GA: Mercer University Press, 1990).

N. T. Wright, *Paul for Everyone: The Pastoral Letters* (Louisville KY: Westminster John Knox, 2003).

PROPER RELATIONSHIPS

1 Timothy 5: 1-7; 6: 1-2, 17-19

Faded Rules

In *The Cider House Rules* (New York: Ballantine, 1985), novelist John Irving focuses our attention on Homer, a boy raised at St. Cloud's Orphanage as the protégé of Dr. Wilbur Larch. When it came time for Homer to leave that safe but confining place, he was hired on to work in an apple orchard. His home became a cider house, where he bunked with the rest of the orchard hands.

One day, as Homer and the others were cleaning and painting the cider house, he found a sheet of thin typing paper tacked to the wall. The type on it was faint from exposure to the sun, but he could see that it was some kind of list. He would have thrown it away, except that the top line caught his attention: "CIDER HOUSE RULES." "What rules?" he wondered as he read down the page:

1. Please don't operate the grinder or the press if you've been drinking.
2. Please don't smoke in bed or use candles.
3. Please don't go up on the roof if you've been drinking—especially at night.
4. Please wash out the press cloths the same day or night they are used.
5. Please remove the rotary screen immediately after you've finished pressing and hose it clean WHEN THE POMACE IS STILL WET ON IT!
6. Please don't take bottles with you when you go up on the roof.
7. Please—even if you are very hot (or if you've been drinking)—don't go into the cold-storage room to sleep.

8. Please give your shopping list to the crew boss by seven o'clock in the morning.
9. There should be no more than half a dozen people on the roof at any one time.
(281–82)

The owners of the cider house wrote the rules the workers were to keep. The issuers of the rules were not the ones who had to abide by them. The rules were mostly concerned about protecting the owners from liability for injuries to their workers and from damage to their property. There wasn't a single word about how the owners would treat the workers or even about how the workers should relate to each other. There was nothing about what to do if a laborer were injured on the job or fell ill during the night. It's no wonder that the rules faded, not just on the page, but from the workers' awareness or compliance.

Rules of the Household

What about our rules? Is it evident that they grow out of understanding of, and compassion for, the conditions under which people live? Do they express mutual responsibility and shared commitments?

Every "house"—every group—has a set of rules, although we might not call them rules. They are the assumptions we make about what a community should be like. They're the expectations we have for how the people should treat and care for one another. Schools, workplaces, professions, and our own families have them. So does God's household, the church.

In our studies of 1 Timothy, we've noted that, like the wider culture of which they were a part, first-century Christians thought of leadership as the management or stewardship of a household. We saw, for instance, the connection Paul made between how prospective leaders functioned in their own families and how they were likely to function in the family of faith: "They should manage their own household well...because if they don't know how to manage their own household, how can they take care of God's church?" (3:4-5).

As part of taking care of God's church, its leaders developed certain "house rules," or, as New Testament scholars often call them, "household codes" (see Col 3:18–4:1; Eph 5:22–6:9; Titus 2:1-10; 1 Pet 2:18–3:7). The passages on which we focus in this lesson are excerpts from one of those codes.

Such codes were common not only in the writings of church leaders, but also in the reflections of rabbis and of Greek and Roman philosophers. They spelled out the obligations members of households (large and small, private and public) had toward each other.

The codes we find in the New Testament are not entirely original compositions by the biblical authors. Instead, they are adaptations and modifications of codes that leaders like Paul borrowed from the wider culture. When Paul revised such codes, the resulting rules reflected more fully than did the norms of the surrounding culture, his—and Jesus'—vision for the freedom, equality, and dignity of all people.

We need to acknowledge, however, that the codes Paul included in his letters sometimes continued to reflect the hierarchical and patriarchal assumptions of his time and place. That acknowledgement is especially important as we interpret, for instance, his instructions about the role of women and the conduct of slaves (see 1 Tim 2:9-15; 6:1-2). When the codes leave unjust patterns of relationship largely unchallenged, we should remember that Paul himself had a more inclusive dream of community in Christ (see Gal 3:26-27; Col 3:9-11), a dream he did not always find it possible to enact. His occasional accommodations of the diverse cultures in which his churches lived are frustrating to us. In my view, those accommodations are also cautionary for us. In what ways do we surrender a kingdom vision of merciful justice in favor of an uneasy peace with our culture?

Guidance for Relationships

The household code Paul addresses to Timothy includes wisdom about relationships with church members of varying ages (5:1-2), with widows who live in diverse conditions (5:3-16), with elders (5:17-22), with slaves and their masters (6:1-2), and with the wealthy (6:17-19). Paul's counsel begins with the expectation that Timothy relate as honorably and lovingly to members of the congregation as he would to members of his own family. He must relate to older men as to his father, to older women as to his mother, to younger men as to his brother, and to younger women as to his sisters. Paul underscored that Timothy's relationships with younger women should be characterized by "appropriate respect" (1 Tim 5:2) or "absolute purity" (NRSV)—a likely reference to the importance of sexual virtue.

In my boyhood church, I heard adults call each other "sister" and "brother." I was taught to call the adults who were my parents' close friends "aunt" and "uncle." These terms helped nurture a congregational climate of mutual respect and love. While we don't often use this overt family language these days, we still have the hope and expectation that our churches will accept, know, and love us as would a welcoming and caring family. Some years ago, a middle-aged man in the First Baptist Church of Asheville said, after he'd suffered through the ordeal of a serious illness, "My church is just like family to me. In fact, I feel closer to the people in my Sunday school class than I do to my own brothers and sisters. I just don't know what I'd do without them." I've heard many other people offer similar affirmations of the love they've received from their church.

Less frequently, but sadly, I've heard people express disappointment that their church hasn't felt like family to them. For a variety of reasons, they've felt overlooked, left out, or let down by the congregations of which they were a part. They didn't experience the closeness, warmth, and support they wanted and needed.

Paul urged Timothy to serve as a model of extending to everyone the honor and love healthy families give to each member. Inevitably over time, the pastoral leaders of a congregation help to set and maintain the tone and patterns of relationship within it.

A particular concern for the church that was determined to be a family was the care it would give to its widows. The overarching principle Paul gave to Timothy was that the church should "take care of widows who are truly needy" (5:3). A commitment to the support of widows was part of the Jewish tradition that was the cradle of Christian faith (see Deut 14:29; 24:17-21; 26:12). It was the unintentional but still hurtful neglect of some widows in the earliest days of the church in Jerusalem that led to the creation of the role of deacon (Acts 6:1-7). James, the brother of Jesus and a leader in that Jerusalem church, said plainly: "True devotion, the kind that is pure and faultless before God the Father, is this: to care for orphans and widows in their difficulties and to keep the world from contaminating us" (Jas 1:27).

Paul distinguished among widows who were of diverse ages and economic circumstances. There were widows who should be able to count on the care of their children and grandchildren. Paul wanted to be sure that these widows' family members honored their rightful obligation to their mothers and grand-mothers (5:4, 7-8). There were widows whose age made it unlikely that they would marry again and who were "all alone" (5:5). There were wealthy widows who had no need for the church's financial support. Some of those well-off widows, who lived in "luxury," drew Paul's ire for their self-centeredness and self-indulgence (5:6).

In verses beyond the focus of today's lesson, Paul gave even more specific instructions for widows who should be enrolled in the church's ministry of ongoing provision (see 5:9-11). He also singled out for corrective instruction some younger widows who had apparently given him reason to think they would take unfair advantage of the church's generosity, use its support to avoid their appropriate responsibilities, and bring embarrassment to the congregation (5:11-15).

The enduring lessons in Paul's counsel to Timothy about the care of widows are twofold: (1) the church has a nonnegotiable obligation to care, in ways that make sense in our time and place, for its vulnerable members; and (2) the church should be wise in allocating resources to the care of the vulnerable so that it's more likely that the people who truly need help are the ones who will receive it.

We've already noted that in his teaching about relationships between slaves and masters (6:1-2), Paul made some unsettling concessions to the wider culture. He didn't challenge the existence of slavery, and he seemed more concerned about the reputation of the church in the eyes of outsiders than about moving more decisively toward the essential equality of all people that he taught in other places. The church's agonizingly slow progress toward the realization that the gospel of Jesus Christ is incompatible with the practice of slavery can, as I've suggested, serve as a warning to us that it is possible to be blinded to injustices of which we are a part. Our culture's dominant values and expectations cast a mesmerizing spell on our imaginations, making it difficult to recognize some of the places and people in whom God's Spirit is now working—often without our cooperation—for liberation, justice, and peace.

Paul urged Timothy to care for the wealthy members of the church by cautioning them not to become "egotistical" and not "to place their hope on their finances" (6:17). It's a caution we need to hear if we find ourselves financially secure and relatively comfortable. In those situations, we can be tempted to forget that, even when we've worked hard to earn whatever we have, the ability to work and earn is a gift from God, "who richly provides everything for our enjoyment" (6:17).

For followers of Jesus, part of the enjoyment of financial resources is the opportunity to be "generous, and to share with others" (6:18). Our hold on money is fleeting, both because it is "uncertain" (6:17), meaning we can lose it even more quickly than we earned it, and because even if we remain well off until the day we die, we've still only managed to keep it for a relatively brief span of time. It's better instead to use money in support of real "treasure" (6:19), which are those ministries and projects that increase the flow of the most enduring virtues: faith, hope, and love (1 Cor 13:13). These virtues characterize abundant and authentic life and are also the heart of the household of faith.

Notes

Notes